MONOPOLY MASTERMIND

Charles B. Darrow

PAIGE V. POLINSKY

**Checkerboard
Library**

An Imprint of Abdo Publishing
abdopublishing.com

abdopublishing.com

Published by Abdo Publishing, a division of ABDO, PO Box 398166, Minneapolis, Minnesota 55439. Copyright © 2018 by Abdo Consulting Group, Inc. International copyrights reserved in all countries. No part of this book may be reproduced in any form without written permission from the publisher. Checkerboard Library™ is a trademark and logo of Abdo Publishing.

Printed in the United States of America, North Mankato, Minnesota
062017
092017

 THIS BOOK CONTAINS
RECYCLED MATERIALS

Design and Production: Mighty Media, Inc.
Editor: Liz Salzmann
Cover Photographs: Courtesy of The Strong®, Rochester, New York (center); Mighty Media, Inc. (border)
Interior Photographs: Alamy, p. 5; AP Images, p. 21; Courtesy of The Strong®, Rochester, New York, pp. 10, 13, 15, 23, 29 (top); iStockphoto, pp. 18, 29 (bottom); Mighty Media, Inc., p. 25; Shutterstock, pp. 7, 12, 25, 26, 27, 28 (all three); Wikimedia Commons, pp. 6, 9, 11, 19

Publisher's Cataloging-in-Publication Data
Names: Polinsky, Paige V., author.
Title: Monopoly mastermind: Charles B. Darrow / by Paige V. Polinsky.
Other titles: Charles B. Darrow
Description: Minneapolis, MN : Abdo Publishing, 2018. | Series: Toy trailblazers |
    Includes bibliographical references and index.
Identifiers: LCCN 2016962799 | ISBN 9781532110955 (lib. bdg.) |
    ISBN 9781680788808 (ebook)
Subjects: LCSH: Darrow, Charles B., 1889-1967--Juvenile literature. | Monopoly
    (Game)--Juvenile literature. | Board game industry--United States--Juvenile
    literature. | Inventors--United States--Biography--Juvenile literature. |
    Toymakers--United States--History--Juvenile literature.
Classification: DDC 794/092 [B]--dc23
LC record available at http://lccn.loc.gov/2016962799

CONTENTS

A Play Sensation 4

The Landlord's Game 6

Play and Pass It On 8

Depression Distraction 10

Darrow's Monopoly 12

Supply and Demand 14

Parker Brothers Purchase 16

Patent Protection 18

Wartime Wonder 20

Monopoly Mischief 22

Monopoly Makers 24

Timeless Tokens 26

Timeline 28

Glossary 30

Websites 31

Index 32

Chapter 1
A PLAY
Sensation

Anyone can be a millionaire for a day. All it takes is a game of Monopoly! Monopoly is the most popular board game in the world. It is played in more than one hundred countries. But how did one board game become a worldwide sensation? It is partly thanks to the resourcefulness and determination of a man named Charles B. Darrow.

Charles was born in Maryland on August 10, 1889. He was an only child. Soon after Charles was born, the Darrows moved to Pennsylvania. There, his father worked as a civil engineer. Little is known about Charles's childhood. As a young adult, he took several classes at the University of Pennsylvania. But he never graduated.

Darrow joined the military during **World War I**. After the war ended in 1918, he worked as a heating engineer. Around this time, Darrow married a woman named Esther. Darrow and Esther settled down in Germantown, Pennsylvania. Many people believe that's where Monopoly

was first created. But that is not entirely true. The board game actually
began in Virginia with a woman named Elizabeth Magie.

Chapter 2

The Landlord's GAME

Elizabeth Magie was a busy, independent woman. She worked as a secretary and an actress. She was also a writer and inventor. Magie felt that greedy **landlords** were ruining the **economy**. She supported the tax reforms proposed by economist Henry George. George believed people should be taxed based on the value of the land they owned. This way, wealthy landlords would pay higher taxes than laborers.

Magie thought a board game would be a fun way to teach people about

Henry George's 1879 book *Progress and Poverty* and other writings inspired Magie's interest in economics.

George's tax theory. In 1903, she created The **Landlord**'s Game. The board had nine spaces on each side. The spaces represented properties.

Players rolled dice and moved pieces around the board. A player who landed on an unowned property could purchase it. If the property was already owned, he or she had to pay rent to the owner. Magie hoped the game would show people how greed hurt others.

Magie tried to sell The Landlord's Game to the Parker Brothers game company. But Parker Brothers thought it was too confusing. And the company didn't think a game about business would sell well. So Magie found a company in New York that helped her publish the game herself.

FUN FACT

Magie owned her own home and didn't marry until she was 44 years old. This was very unusual for a woman in the early 1900s.

Chapter 3

PLAY AND
Pass It On

The **Landlord**'s Game wasn't an instant hit. But over time, its popularity grew. However, it did not have the effect that Magie had hoped. Most players didn't care about the welfare of other players. Instead, they eagerly collected as much money as they could. Magie's anti-greed message was left behind.

Soon, people started making their own **versions** of The Landlord's Game. The game was more fun when players recognized the names of the properties. So, people created games related to their own cities. The properties in these versions were labeled with local locations.

Economics professors shared the game with their students. Students from various colleges made an important change to the game. They grouped the properties into sets. A player who owned a whole set had a monopoly. If a player owned a monopoly, he or she could charge higher rents to anyone landing on a monopoly property.

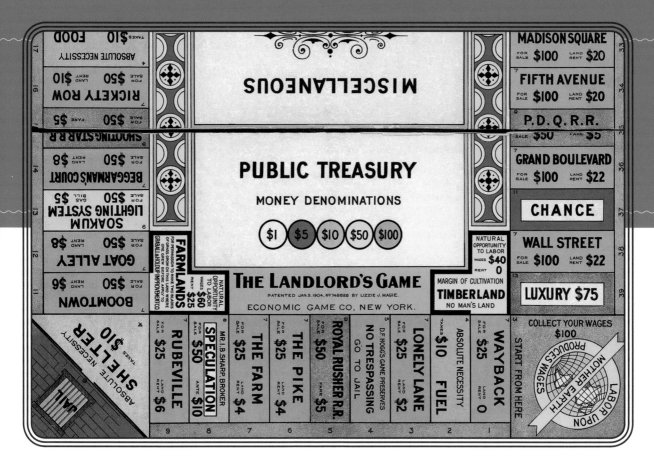

The Landlord's Game was first published in 1906 by the Economic Game Company of New York, a company created by Magie and others with similar views.

Charles Darrow first saw a copy of The **Landlord**'s Game in 1931. His and Esther's friends Charles and Olive Todd had one. The Todds taught the Darrows how to play it. Their game was a **version** from Atlantic City, New Jersey. But while they played, Darrow saw more than a fun party game. He saw a life-changing opportunity.

Chapter 4

DEPRESSION
Distraction

The time the Darrows were learning The **Landlord**'s Game was during the **Great Depression**. In 1929, the US **stock market** had crashed. Companies began failing and had to fire their workers. By 1933, up to 15 million people were unemployed. Darrow was one of them. He had lost his job as a heating engineer soon after the crash.

Esther supported the family by working in a weaving studio. Meanwhile, Darrow took any

FUN FACT

During the Great Depression, one of Darrow's odd jobs was as a part-time dog walker.

President Franklin Delano Roosevelt created relief programs that gave the unemployed money and food during the Great Depression. But people had to wait in line for hours.

odd job he could find. But after three years, he was tired of worrying about money. He discovered playing The **Landlord**'s Game for a few hours gave him a much-needed break. It was a short vacation from reality. In a time where many people could not afford basic groceries, Darrow and his friends competed for expensive real estate. The money they threw around was fake. But it sure felt good!

Darrow fell in love with The Landlord's Game. Like many players before him, he decided to make a **version** of his own. He asked the Todds for a copy of the Atlantic City game and the rules. After playing the game several more times, Darrow got to work.

Chapter 5

Darrow's
MONOPOLY

Darrow was full of enthusiasm for the game. He couldn't wait to produce his own. But first he needed to gather the proper materials. He bought a sheet of **oilcloth**. Then Darrow carefully copied the Atlantic City streets in the Todds' game onto the oilcloth. This was the game's board.

Creating the board was just the beginning. Darrow then used a typewriter to create each playing card and rule sheet. He copied the rules from the Todds' game as well.

Instead of including game pieces, Darrow suggested that players use items they have on hand. These could be things such as bottle caps, buttons, and coins. Finally, Darrow carved tiny houses and hotels out of scrap wood. It took a full day to create a single game.

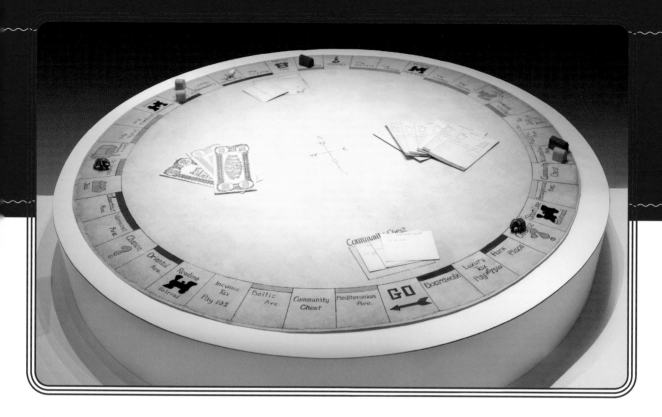

The original round Monopoly board was designed to fit a dining room table.
The whole family could sit around the table and play together!

Darrow could construct the board on his own. But he wanted an
artist to make it look amazing. Luckily, his friend Franklin Alexander was
a cartoonist. Alexander worked with Darrow to decorate the game. He
added more color to the board. He also drew expressive characters on the
cards. Now the game was more than just playable. It was a work of art!
Darrow called his game Monopoly.

Chapter 6
SUPPLY and Demand

Monopoly was a huge hit with Darrow's friends and family. Many of them wanted their own copies. Darrow realized his game could make him big money! He gathered more materials and made more copies of the game. He continued to use Atlantic City locations to label the spaces. Darrow sold them for $2 each. As the demand for Monopoly grew, Darrow became flooded with orders. He couldn't create enough sets all by himself.

Darrow hired printer Lytton Patterson Jr. With Patterson's help, Darrow no longer had to draw each board by hand. Instead, the boards were printed on a printing press.

Darrow brought his game to John Wanamaker's. Wanamaker's was a department store in Pennsylvania. The store agreed to

FUN FACT

Parker Brothers sent Darrow a rejection letter that claimed that Monopoly had 52 major problems.

Nobody had ever seen a game like the 1934 version of Monopoly. With its bright colors and charming design, people saw it as a work of art!

purchase 500 Monopoly sets. They sold out quickly! Darrow realized he needed the help of a bigger **distributor**. So, in 1934, he presented Monopoly to two game companies, Parker Brothers and Milton Bradley.

Unfortunately, neither company was interested in the game. They said it took too long to play and was too **complicated**. Nevertheless, the demand for Monopoly was greater than ever. So, Darrow and Patterson continued to fill the orders as best they could.

Chapter 7

Parker Brothers
PURCHASE

By Christmas 1934, Monopoly was at the top of many wish lists. Times were still tough. But for many people, $2 was a reasonable price for hours of enjoyment! Darrow received many orders for Monopoly. Department stores and toy stores placed huge orders of their own. Darrow worked constantly, overseeing the production and packaging of every Monopoly set.

Eventually, Parker Brothers changed its opinion of the game. It saw that Monopoly was successful and popular. The company paid Darrow $7,000 for the rights to publish and sell his game.

Parker Brothers began producing Monopoly in March 1935. Company executives were still concerned about the game's length. So, they

FUN FACT

Monopoly's famous **mascot** is known as Mr. Monopoly. But his official name is Rich Uncle Pennybags!

added rules for a shorter **version** of the game. They also included metal game pieces instead of having players find items to use. Early tokens included a cannon, an iron, a top hat, and a boot.

Within one month, Parker Brothers was producing more than 20,000 sets each week. The company printed the game 24 hours a day to keep up with orders. After years of struggling through the **Great Depression**, Parker Brothers was beginning to be profitable again. And it was all thanks to a game they had once rejected.

Chapter 8

PATENT
Protection

The demand for Monopoly showed no signs of slowing. With the company's help, Darrow patented the game on December 31, 1935. Now nobody else could sell Darrow's **version** of the game. But various versions of The **Landlord**'s Game were still around.

Parker Brothers didn't want to lose any business to these other games. The company made deals with the game owners. Parker Brothers paid the owners for the patents to their games. Elizabeth Magie received $500 for The Landlord's Game.

Charles Darrow was a millionaire when he retired in 1935. He was also a national legend. Many believed that Darrow was the

Darrow's patent for Monopoly was approved in just four months. This was a very short time for patents in the United States.

game's sole inventor. Unfortunately, Darrow did not correct this misunderstanding. When asked how he thought up the game, he said the idea just came to him. He did not mention having been inspired by The **Landlord**'s Game.

By 1936, two million Monopoly sets had sold. But few people knew about Magie. She was hurt and upset. She felt cheated by Parker Brothers. But the company supported Darrow's claims. His rags-to-riches **Depression** story was popular and inspirational. Most importantly, it sold more games.

Chapter 9

WARTIME
Wonder

Selling Monopoly to Parker Brothers made Darrow a very wealthy man. He moved his family to a farm in Bucks County, Pennsylvania. There, Charles and Esther grew rare orchids. The family vacationed all over the world together. Their days of poverty were long behind them.

However, life was gloomier for the world at large. **World War II** had started in 1939. During the war, thousands of **Allied** soldiers were captured by the Germans. The British Secret Intelligence Service (SIS) had a plan to help Allied prisoners escape. The SIS asked John Waddington Ltd. to help carry out the plan.

John Waddington Ltd. was a British company that produced Monopoly sets sold outside of the United States. The company also printed maps for British pilots. John Waddington Ltd. created

FUN FACT

The longest Monopoly game ever played lasted 70 straight days.

"Special **Edition** Monopoly" games. The workers hid a compass, metal file, and escape map in each game.

The **Allies** delivered the games to prison camps in aid packages. The packages also included food and other supplies. The Germans accepted the packages because they were having trouble getting enough food for the prisoners. The aid packages from the Allies solved this problem. By the time the war ended, more than 35,000 Allied soldiers had escaped from German prison camps. Many of them owed their freedom to Monopoly!

Chapter 10
MONOPOLY
Mischief

Monopoly's popularity continued through the 1950s. But not everybody was a fan. The leaders of **communist** countries including Cuba, China, and the **USSR** banned the game. Monopoly was based on people buying, selling, and renting property. Communism doesn't allow people to do this. These governments feared Monopoly would inspire their citizens to revolt. So, they forbid anyone from playing it.

Meanwhile, on August 28, 1967, Charles Darrow died. Monopoly continued to live on, but not without problems. In 1973, an **economics** professor named Ralph Anspach created a board game of his own. After playing Monopoly with his son, he was inspired to create a new board game. Its goal was to show the dangers of **capitalism**. He called it Anti-Monopoly.

FUN FACT

Russia's Monopoly ban was lifted in 1987. But the game is still banned in North Korea and Cuba.

Parker Brothers was very upset with Anspach's game. In 1974, the company **sued** him for using the Monopoly **trademark** without **permission**. But Anspach wouldn't back down. He carefully researched the board game's history. While doing so, he uncovered Elizabeth Magie's story.

Magie had been long forgotten. But Anspach used her story to argue his case. He showed that the game had existed before Parker Brothers bought it. For this reason, their trademark shouldn't count. The case dragged on for years. But in 1983, Anspach won. Like "chess" or "checkers," the word "monopoly" was officially free to use.

Chapter 11

MONOPOLY
Makers

Monopoly lovers can still buy the classic game of their childhood. But not everyone is interested in Atlantic City, New Jersey. Luckily, there are now more than 300 other **versions** for them to play!

There are Monopoly **editions** for many major cities around the world. Sports fans can play Monopoly editions based on their favorite teams. Students can play Monopoly versions of their own universities. There are even Monopoly boards about music stars, movies, and TV shows!

No matter the edition, most Monopoly sets are made the same way. But much has changed since Charles Darrow hand drew game boards in his home. A system of huge machines and busy employees work around the clock.

FUN FACT

A standard Monopoly set comes with $20,580 in Monopoly money.

1 MONOPOLY GAME BOARD $20,580 IN MONOPO[L]

16 CHANCE CARDS ·················   28 TITLE DE[ED]

16 COMMUNITY CHEST CARDS

1 INSTRUCTION BOOKLET   2 SIX-SIDED

12 PLASTIC HOTELS 32 PLASTIC HOUSES 9 META[L]

Chapter 12

Timeless TOKENS

Today, Parker Brothers is owned by toy and game company Hasbro. And while Monopoly is more than 80 years old, Hasbro has kept it fresh and modern. In 2008, Hasbro released a Monopoly game for **smartphones**.

The next year, Hasbro teamed up with Google Maps to release Monopoly City Streets. Players could purchase and construct virtual buildings all over the world. It became one of the most popular **online** games in the United States.

Hasbro has also used **social media** to its advantage. In 2013, they held a Save Your Token campaign. Monopoly enthusiasts got to decide which game token Hasbro would replace. And they could suggest what the new token should be.

A life-size Monopoly board was created in London for the London Games Festival in 2016. People rolled digital dice on their smartphones and then walked around the board!

Anyone who wanted to do this could visit Monopoly's Facebook page and vote. People from more than 185 different countries voted on the Monopoly tokens. In the end, a cat ended up replacing the iron. After this, Monopoly sales rose **dramatically**.

Today, more than 250 million Monopoly sets have been sold around the world. Charles Darrow did not build this empire on his own. But his determination and ambition made it the game sensation that it is today!

TIMELINE

1889
Charles B. Darrow is born in Maryland on August 10.

1914–1918
Darrow fights in World War I.

1931
Darrow learns The Landlord's Game from the Todds. He creates Monopoly in its image.

COMMUNITY CHEST

FOLLOW INSTRUCTIONS ON TOP CARD

1903
Elizabeth Magie creates a board game called The Landlord's Game.

1918
Darrow begins working as a heating engineer.

1934
The Parker Brothers and Milton Bradley toy companies reject Monopoly.

1935
Darrow successfully sells Monopoly to Parker Brothers. He then retires.

1967
Charles Darrow dies on August 28.

2009
Monopoly City Streets becomes one of the most popular online games in the United States.

1950s
Monopoly is banned in communist countries including Cuba, China, and the USSR.

1983
The word "monopoly" loses its trademark.

2013
The Save Your Token campaign increases Monopoly sales.

Glossary

allies – people, groups, or nations united for some special purpose. During World War II, Great Britain, France, the United States, and the Soviet Union were called the Allies.

capitalism – an economic system where businesses compete to sell their products and services.

communism – a social and economic system in which everything is owned by the government and given to the people as needed. A person who believes in communism is called a communist.

complicated – hard to understand, explain, or deal with.

distributor – a company that sells products to stores.

dramatically – very noticeably.

economy – the way a nation produces and uses goods, services, and natural resources. Economics is the study of the economy. An economist is an expert in economics.

edition – a special issue or version of a product.

Great Depression – the period from 1929 to 1942 of worldwide economic trouble. There was little buying or selling, and many people could not find work.

landlord – a person who owns houses or apartments and rents them to other people.

mascot – a person, animal, or object that is supposed to bring good luck to a team or an organization.

oilcloth – cloth treated with oil or paint to make it waterproof.

online – connected to the Internet.

permission – formal consent.

smartphone – a mobile phone that can connect to the Internet.

social media – forms of electronic communication in which users share information, ideas, photos, and personal messages. Facebook and Twitter are examples of social media.

stock market – a place where stocks and bonds, which represent parts of businesses, are bought and sold.

sue – to bring legal action against a person or an organization.

trademark – something such as a word that identifies a certain company. It cannot be used by others without permission.

USSR – Union of Soviet Socialist Republics. The USSR was a country in Europe and Asia from 1922 to 1991.

version – a different form or type of an original.

World War I – from 1914 to 1918, fought in Europe. Great Britain, France, Russia, the United States, and their allies were on one side. Germany, Austria-Hungary, and their allies were on the other side.

World War II – from 1939 to 1945, fought in Europe, Asia, and Africa. Great Britain, France, the United States, the Soviet Union, and their allies were on one side. Germany, Italy, Japan, and their allies were on the other side.

Alexander, Franklin, 13
Anspach, Ralph, 22, 23
Anti-Monopoly, 22, 23
Atlantic City, 9, 11, 12, 14, 24

bans against Monopoly, 22
birthplace, 4

Darrow, Esther, 4, 9, 10, 20

early years, 4, 5
economics, 6, 8, 22

game production, 12, 13, 14, 15, 16, 17, 24, 25
game sales, 14, 15, 16, 17, 18, 19, 20, 27
game tokens, 12, 17, 26, 27
game versions, 8, 9, 11, 17, 18, 24

George, Henry, 6, 7
Germantown, Pennsylvania, 4
Great Depression, 10, 11, 17, 19
greed, 6, 7, 8

Hasbro, 26

John Waddington Ltd., 20, 21

Landlord's Game, The, 7, 8, 9, 10, 11, 18, 19

Magie, Elizabeth, 5, 6, 7, 8, 9, 18, 19, 23
Maryland, 4
Monopoly City Streets, 26

Parker Brothers, 7, 15, 16, 17, 18, 19, 20, 23, 26
patent, 18, 19
Patterson, Lytton, Jr., 14, 15
Pennsylvania, 4, 14, 20

rejection, 15, 17
retirement, 18, 20

social media campaign, 26, 27
struggles, 10, 11

Todd, Charles and Olive, 9, 11, 12
trademark, 23

Virginia, 5

World War I, 4
World War II, 20, 21